D0743583

Sufism and Islam

Other books in the Sufism Lecture Series:

Sufism

Sufism and Wisdom

Sufism and Knowledge

Sufism and Peace

Sufism
and
Islam

Molana Salaheddin Ali Nader Shah Angha
"Pir Oveyssi"

Sorbonne University
April 3, 1995

M.T.O. SHAHMAGHSOUDI® PUBLICATIONS

M.T.O. SHAHMAGHSOUDI® PUBLICATIONS

Angha, Salaheddin Ali Nader Shah

Sufism and Islam

Library of Congress Catalog Card Number: 95-077983
ISBN: 0-910735-97-2

First edition: 1996
Second edition: 1997

Printed in the U.S.A.

Published and distributed by M.T.O. Shahmaghsoudi
5225 Wisconsin Ave., N.W.   Suite #502
Washington, D.C. 20015
U.S.A.

website: http://mto.shahmaghsoudi.org

Contents

Wherever the masculine gender is used, it is solely for the purpose of linguistic convenience. Since the intent of religion is for the spiritual elevation of each individual, we believe that religion addresses the soul, and the soul is not subject to gender classification.

Introduction

A few years ago Hazrat Pir began one of his lectures by asking the audience these questions, "If there were only one in the world, and that one were you, what would be your name? Who would you be? Would you hate? Would you love?" Only an instant lapsed before he calmly asked, "If there were one, and that one had all the knowledge of the universe, and could respond to all your needs and all your wants, what would you do?" Then he said, Sufism is about this "ONE".

Hazrat Pir's method of teaching is definitely thought provoking, and his students say demanding and challenging. Some say he evokes the same system of learning as Socrates did with his students. Those who have interviewed him usually confess that they are totally disarmed by his questions, becoming engaged in an intense learning experience. True to his mission, Hazrat Pir never ceases to teach. His main goal is to show people how they may attain the true state of human dignity, peace and tranquility. His definition of the human being rises above social, cultural and psychological definitions.

Sophisticated communication systems have linked people worldwide, breaking down the "absolutes" that societies, communities and countries had defined and kept sacred for themselves. It is the age of relativity. While exposure to diversity has expanded people's vision of the world, it has also brought elements of insecurity and instability into the day-to-day life of many people. When standards collapse and values shift, where can we find the ultimate definition of our "self"?

Hazrat Pir says, "Each person is a complex and unique masterpiece." Most people, if not all, would like this statement to be true. But what prevents us from experiencing it? What must happen for us to even understand the magnitude of this statement? If we don't allow our imagination to quickly define it, package it and file it away, we could start on a powerful journey of self-realization, which would change the entire fabric of societies, human interactions and legal and social systems. This means moving through the multidimensional patterns of social conditionings that have structured our lives, formed our identities, personalities, self-worth, our perceptions of others and our value systems.

How can we put these aside? And if we should put them aside what would be the yardstick with which we could measure our achievements, our knowledge and our understanding of anything?

Hazrat Pir says, "You are the measure for everything." He is often heard saying, "You have everything that you need. All you need to do is to lift the boundaries you have created, then 'reality' will unveil." But if one wants to be this "unique masterpiece", how, realistically, does one "lift the boundaries?"

"Know thyself," wrote the philosopher Plato about integrity; because "an unexamined life is not worth living." From the time of the Greeks, Western philosophy has advocated self-knowledge — internal learning. Internal learning is at the heart of Islam. As the Holy Prophet Muhammad has said, "Whoever knows the true self knows God."

To begin at the beginning — know thyself. The "i", the individual, is a cherished concept, the acknowledged foundation upon which democracy is built. By transforming the "i", one can go a long way towards transforming the greater world in which the "i" lives. The belief in the perfectibility of the Self has strengthened the fiber of Western society and the collapse of this belief in the twentieth century has brought about alienation and uncertainty in modern societies. Untouched by today's social, economic and political shifts, Hazrat Pir represents a strong and clear voice, reminding us of the urgency to know the true and stable "I". In so doing, he reaffirms the human being's capacity to master the self.

One of the significant contributions of Hazrat Pir to the reservoir of world knowledge is the idea that, because the world has projected its divisions and boundaries onto the vulnerable "i", one must create a process for achieving mastery of mind. This is done by first removing these divisions and boundaries onto the "i" through an inner experience of religion that begins with spiritual integration and ends with a complete metamorphosis. It is no coincidence that two of the healthiest and strongest mystical minds of the Catholic tradition — St. John of the Cross and St. Teresa of Avila — learned much about their mystical journey from Islam as it was received into the Spanish Moorish tradition.

Much can be learned from the way Hazrat Pir teaches. Ideally, a student should think: "I will commit myself not to the idea but the process of mastering my own mind and if enough of us do the same 'the world' will simultaneously change because 'the world' is us." A simple way of stating a complicated process, but it is a beginning.

This series of essays, scripts of lectures given by Hazrat Pir discusses his teaching as it relates to the history of Sufism, peace, wisdom, knowledge, healing, meditation, love, prayer, balance, and alchemy. The author, Hazrat Pir Molana Salaheddin Ali Nader Shah Angha, is the forty-second master of Maktab Tarighat Oveyssi Shahmaghsoudi *(School of Islamic Sufism)*, a school that traces its lineage back to the very advent of Islam in the seventh century A.D. While Hazrat Pir's lectures are faithful to the tradition which produced him and which he now guides, they also reflect the mark he has made on that tradition. Raised and trained in the esoteric tradition of Sufism and educated in the West, Hazrat Pir is exceptionally sensitive to the modern world. Accomplished in the disciplines of religion, science, philosophy and poetry, and trained by his father, Molana Hazrat Shah Maghsoud Sadegh Angha (Professor Angha), himself a great master of Sufism and an advanced physicist, Hazrat Pir has, from a very young age developed not only a perceptive and accomplished mind, but also an expansive spirit.

Our desire to transform the world, he teaches, must begin with a transformation of "i" into "I", the true Self. To the Sufi, this necessitates a dialogue between heart and mind. What Westerners call internal learning, or self-knowledge is, to the Sufi, more like a glorified "i" short of a transformation into Self. For example, Hazrat Pir teaches that drug addiction, the scourge of modern society, will elude well-meaning people's attempts to eradicate it, until they understand how to heal the mind of its addiction, and discover the stable "I". To heal the mind of its addiction, one must acknowledge that God, and not the ego is at the center of the "I". Only then is one capable of living a healthy and balanced life.

A serious scrutiny of Hazrat Pir's example would serve the purpose of welcoming a science of mind that may well complement the existing one in the West. Islam is much in the news these days and concerned people want to know more about a culture that is at once alien and familiar — as familiar as the lines from the *Holy Qur'an,* "I am closer to you than your jugular vein." Most Westerners would not have ever read these words unless they were familiar with a poem of the same name by French writer James Sacré. Yet there is a certain basic sanity about those words rooted in a deeper source than that of the creative ego. Heirs of the Greek tradition, the West is only beginning to realize why the heart of Islam seems so close — it has always been there, part of its world, part of its culture, part of its "I" from the beginning.

So it seems fitting that on American soil, a nation founded on the spirit of exploration and discovery, Hazrat Pir has designed and built a memorial in memory of his teacher and father, Professor Angha. In three dimensions, near Novato, California stands a wonderful metaphor for 1400 years of spiritual labor and the integration of the human being's consciousness. There in architecture and here in words on the page, Hazrat Pir encourages the seeker to submit to his or her own metamorphosis and flower like the art of the memorial through the integration of Self, through integrity to the final union with God.

Sufism
and
Islam

In the Name of God
Most Gracious, Most Merciful

*P*raise to the All Merciful Lord who has manifested the universe, and upon the wisdom of the *Holy Qur'an*, then created man to sustain cognition and to declare that wisdom through faith and submission. Praise to the "One" who expands unity to encompass all beings, who nurtures truth in the midst of all expression, and who grants enlightenment to his worshippers' early morning pleas.

In following the blessed command of God in the *Holy Qur'an (57:7)*, "And spend (in charity) out of the (substance) whereof He has made you Heirs.", it is my intention to express the essence of metaphysical revelations and scientific explorations using the simplest explanations. In accord with the laws of nature which guide every single sound wave to its awaiting capable receiver, may the truth of these teachings find their expectant capable receivers transcending the barriers of time, place, language, prejudice, and superstition. May this conveyance of understanding demolish the wall of misinterpretation and ignorance that has separated the physical and metaphysical sciences. May the true seeker find his way to the ultimate truth freely, without the bondage of blind faith, superstition, preconceived bias and supposition.

"Irfan", or Sufism, reveals itself through time; in each era, in its own unique way. It is neither confined by words nor restrained by social customs. It is the practical approach to "gnosis" which means knowledge of "Self". The School of Islamic Sufism provides the path to recognizing one's true "Self", preventing one from going astray by showing how materialistic bonds and attachments prevent humans from experiencing the more elevated states of their existence.

In this brief presentation, my purpose is to present the true meaning of one or two topics, i.e. to expand on the reality of these topics rather than relying on assumed social definitions.

In this era, especially with the advent of instantaneous global communication, it seems as though the metaphysical sciences are perceived as mythical or superfluous pastimes. Most people perceive the teachings of the Prophets in this inept manner. If the views which are presented differ somewhat from their own preconceived ideologies, they are interpreted as fanatic or backward. Or, if their main interest is politics and economics, they are likely to interpret religious beliefs as a source of demonic actions and terrorism. Such superficial interpretations have led to the fabrication of new "religions" as a means of supporting the political and economic demands of a particular group or to cover the ignorance of another. Such manufactured "religions", and their references to historic, poetic and mystical anecdotes have become the criteria for acceptance or rejection of God's teachings.

The traditional way of giving a speech is to express an idea using terminology which seems familiar, but whose truth has not yet been revealed. By using such terminology or repeating the interpretations of famous philosophers, past or present, the speaker ultimately seeks to impose his views on the audience or gain their acceptance. This brings to mind the example of a child's composition in which the student expounds on the topic of "spring" using his own unattained wishes and dreams, repeating others' quotations, and drawing a picture of "spring" based on what was in his mind. Needless to say, the spring that nature presents is far different from that which is described by the child.

To comprehend the essence of a topic, one needs to return and refer to its origin, and not to the marginal notes surrounding it. He who experiences thirst seeks water, and is not concerned with the container. If a man is hungry, he strives to find food, and is not distracted by the plate and the garnishings. If one suffers from an ailment, one searches for the cure, and does not focus on the mood of the physician or the taste of the medicine. Likewise, if a person is attempting to gain knowledge in a field of science, it should be the essence of that knowledge and the humanitarian outcome of it that is foremost in his mind, and not the social status and financial gain it may offer. Such must be the devotion of one who is a seeker of truth and of the reality of existence. He too must return and refer to existence itself, instead of philosophical arguments, mystical stories, superficial traditions, social customs or socio-economic and political propaganda and aspirations.

> Principles that are used in limitation are not the
> means for the discovery of the infinite.[1]

A brief look at the course of science throughout history shows that there was once a time when all sciences were studied together and were collectively called "wisdom". The interested student could study biology, mathematics, and the metaphysical sciences simultaneously. There was a generality in "wisdom" that any researcher who could gather any degree of information, however deficient, could focus upon and address. Since this approach did not produce any real solutions, there was a gradual change starting about 3000 years ago. During the time of Democritus, Socrates, Plato, and finally Aristotle, the debates and conflict of ideas resulted in the expansion of science from an abstract form to a detailed one. Hence, in our present period, each science has branched out into specialized research fields.

Scholars and scientists of physics and its derivatives attempt to discover the governing laws of nature and the hidden capacities of particles, in order to facilitate and optimize the living conditions of man.

Biologists study organisms and by unveiling each membrane and each layer of the manifestations of existence, attempt to get a glimpse of the source of life. They have broken the genetic code of many organisms and are trying to read the human genetic code. By accessing the genetic instructions for the formation of organisms, they seek to reprogram and reshape their properties and traits in ways that will most benefit mankind. Be it for pharmaceutical, medical, nutritional, or other objectives, scientists are seeking and finding ways to optimally utilize whatever nature has offered.

Researchers in the field of psychology and its related branches attempt to observe and define a person's behaviors and reactions as a social entity. In trying to understand thought processes of the mind, they aspire to improve the dynamics of relationships between people, thus making them better suited for society.

These and many other fields of science resemble different branches of a tree. Although each branch presents its own growth and has a place of its own, there is one trunk that they all grow from and there was one seed that opened itself into these magnificent presentations.

In the study of all sciences, it is the reality of man's "self" which is forever seeking, searching in curiosity, with that inward vision and quest for knowledge which is the seed of all sciences. The driving force behind man's quest for revealing the hidden truth beneath the disguises and for surpassing the limitations forced upon him by nature, is his inherent, infinite identity. It is that innate "I" who searches and researches everything from a particle to the universe, embracing all knowledge that is to be discovered. So, the origin and source of all sciences, physical or metaphysical, is the self or "I". It is not any wonder that therein also lies the ultimate goal and purpose of all these researches and scientific explorations.

What is *"irfan"* (Sufism)? It is the path to knowing this "true self". It is cognition of this entity in its absolute form, with all its attributes and capabilities. This is the reality of religion and the essence of God's teachings conveyed through the Prophets. This is *"irfan"*. The Holy Prophet Muhammad (peace and blessings upon him) has said in the *Nahj-ol Fissaha*, "Knowledge is not in the skies to descend upon you, nor is it in the earth to grow for you, but it is hidden within you."

Clearly, this is the reason for the importance of Sufism in the progress and ultimate achievements of science.

Unless the human being is recognized in his totality as an absolute being, with all of his capacities in every stage of his existence, all efforts to discover and capture the hidden aspects of nature will be deemed insufficient and deficient.

Just as there is a process for properly using and displaying a jewel — one must first discover its true value by removing all the layers of dirt and impurities, and sculpting it so that the sun is reflected from each and every angle. In the same manner, the human being must find his own true "value", his inherent identity. He too must remove all earthly bonds that imprison his soul, purify from all impurities, and free himself of all material attributes such as his environment, his society, his possessions, his thoughts, his needs, etc. Only after purification of "I" from whatever else there is, can we achieve cognition. This is the only way to provide the perfect surroundings and environment for the true human being.

Molana Shah Maghsoud Sadegh Angha has said in *The Principles of Faghr and Sufism*:

> The human being in its varying completeness of physical and metaphysical aptitudes can be defined from the savage and beastly level of his primitive ancestors, to the level of intellectuals, discoverers, researchers, to the rank of gnostics and to the exalted state of prophethood, and to the state of annihilation and eternal existence in God. That is to say, what degree and rank, and what stage of innate individual stability he has

reached, which in effect reflect the characteristics of that genuine capability at the stage of individual talent.

The gravest error would be to classify the vast and noble realm of the human being, like other creatures, in the framework of limited thoughts — physical form, environmental needs and changing nature — when, his ascending and noble rank which is drawn in Existence, consists of various stages starting from humanity *(insaniat)* to *(adamiat)* divinity. The universe presented before the human being, which in scientific measurements is infinite, is the perceived image of his own inner infinite existence.[2]

This is why the teachings of *irfan* (Sufism), which is the reality of religion, is free of superficial interpretations, suppositions, ignorance, and blind faith. Unfortunately, these appear to be the building blocks and driving forces of most churches, mosques, and synagogues.

The word *irfan* means gnosis. This concept has been used in the mathematical, biological, and physical sciences, indicating in-depth research into the reality of each subject. For instance, when the phrase "mathematical gnosis" is used, it means that the researcher has stepped beyond the ordinary boundaries of mathematics and is seeking to find the reality of it. But the definition of gnosis particularly refers to religious gnosis. The *arif* (Sufi) is he who has attained knowledge of the reality of religion. If the purpose of scientific work is to reveal the truth that is hidden and illuminate the meaning of life, we can logically conclude that science and *irfan* (Sufism) are the same.

It is apparent that if someone does a vast amount of work researching the life and accomplishments of a mathematician, even if his research is entirely accurate, detailed, and as close to reality as possible, no one would call the researcher a mathematician. It is of utmost importance that we realize that the same is true in the metaphysical sciences. Even if someone studies the classical forms of *irfan*, researches the life of the Sufis, and writes extensive volumes regarding the philosophy, writings, and lifestyles of the Sufis, he himself has not attained the state of self cognition, and the title of Sufi would be false and inaccurate for him.

The same analogy can be used to clarify another misunderstood point which might otherwise mislead an eager seeker of truth. It is clear that repeating Einstein's equation expressing relativity ($E=mc^2$) as many times as possible, or chanting or proclaiming it, would not lead the speaker to experience the state of realization and discovery attained by Einstein. A person who merely repeats the teachings of the Prophets, and uses the philosophy and terminology of Sufism, cannot achieve the state of enlightenment, nor will he experience cognition. He would be lacking the wisdom and knowledge of the Sufi.

As inept and facetious as it seems, if we observe our own attitude and behavior toward metaphysical subjects, it becomes apparent that this is exactly the behavior we engage in. People may pretend to know about existence, gnosis, and the meaning of life, but their lifestyles indicate they are far from cognition. The only thing they recognize as the state of "enlightenment" is their philosophical arguments and undefined vocabulary. "Knowledge based on physical observation is the greatest veil in the discovery of truth."[3]

Another factor which may prevent a seeker from attaining higher levels of revelation and discovery in both metaphysical and physical sciences is substitution of other people's acquisitions and discoveries in place of personal and inherent insight and creativity. In one of his interviews Albert Einstein stated: "It is almost a miracle that modern teaching methods have not entirely strangled the holy curiosity of inquiry."[4]

It is unfortunate that a faulty system of education is forcing eager students to spend most of their time memorizing and repeating the findings of great men of science. Instead they could be encouraged to refer to and search for their own identity and to present their personal creativity. Unless it is clarified for the seeker that the discoveries and teachings of esteemed scholars, past or present, must only be used as an introduction, a stepping stone to his own research and inquiry, he may be doomed to a destiny of forever carrying in his mind the work and ideas of others, unaware of his own potentials. He would resemble a spring of water which has accumulated excessive debris on its fountainhead. Soon, the water that is held back and blocked will become stagnant and lose its ability to give refreshment and life. This is why it is constantly emphasized to the seeker that memorizing and carrying other people's ideologies and revelations will cause hindrance and impede him on his journey of self-cognition.

The *salik* is a seeker who transcends the various stages in his journey to discover the truth. Through repentance he returns from the path of disunity and absorption in desires he has taken in his life, back to heaven, the totality and unity of his true identity. In this journey each layer of earthly bondage is removed and the seeker experiences and resides in the ultimate state of tranquility and harmony.

Practical Sufism is based on conscious awareness: that which is inherent and pure in every human being. Philosophical Sufism is based on deduction and reasoning of the mind. The seeker who practices Sufism learns to control and stop the chattering of his mind in order to eliminate mental deductions, illusions, and imaginings that have no relevance on the truth of his being. This is the only way to experience reality as it truly exists.

Philosophical Sufism uses sensory perceptions, thought processes, and mental deductions. It is therefore limited to the relative comparisons of things, a process which is far from absolute. Since reality is beyond the scope of limited sensory perceptions, comparisons and the conventional arrangements that we create in our minds, it is emphasized to the seeker that on this journey he should concentrate and meditate, controlling the senses and stopping the wanderings of the mind.

As was mentioned earlier, the basis and source of science is the inquiring soul, the creative "self" that breaks through the mind's limitations and steps beyond the social and cultural norms in order to discover the unknown. Sufism is the cognition of this inquisitve soul and creative self. Sufism is the essence of religion and the reality of the teachings of the Prophets. It is not based on interpretations nor blind faith. The true meaning of science is the discovery of truth and the genuine application of all the creative forces within the human being, above and beyond what is interpreted by others.

Therefore, it seems obvious that to achieve an all-encompassing success, one must utilize science and Sufism together. The seeker, an individual who has risen in search of truth, seeking to experience the reality of it, resembles a bird who needs the two wings of science and Sufism, working in harmony and stability, to experience flying in the kingdom of "Self".

Thus, it is clear that exploration and cognition of truth requires a return from the level of philosophy and words which are the domain of comprehension, to the state of truth, which is the realm of revelation. As God states in the *Holy Qur'an*, "Everything will perish but His Face." *(28:88)*, "Thus seek the path leading to Allah." *(9:20)*

It is essential for the researcher to unveil the hidden and eliminate any uncertainty. The seeker is he who reveals reality and establishes himself in it. Then the truth in all its aspects and angles is uncovered. He becomes the knowledgeable one, or as it is sometimes said, enlightened. As is stated in the *Holy Qur'an*: "When the Event Inevitable cometh to pass."*(56:1)* "And verily Judgment and Justice must indeed come to pass." *(51:6)*

It may be necessary at this point to expand on the meaning of what has already been discussed, and explain the meaning of the words that will follow. For instance, let us examine the words, "comprehend" and "comprehension". What is meant by comprehension is an explanation of something as perceived by our senses, an elaboration of its reflected image engraved in the brain. Relative comparisons between these man-made images result in comprehension. Revelation is not based on constructed images and limited perceptions, therefore one cannot use comparisons with it. Comprehension is a series of actions and reactions that are derived from external observations of an object. Whatever we comprehend by observing an object is something that is recognizable by our senses. For example, the sun — we encounter its activity, but this is not the reality of the sun. We cannot comprehend the distance, the actual heat, or the size of it. The instruments man uses to comprehend are his five senses, his mind, his memory, and whatever symbolic image is preserved in his brain as a result of repetitious encounters. What's more, this process is not based on one's own creativity, choice, or will, but rather one's comprehension of subjects is derived from what one's society, family, traditions, and ideologies of the past have constructed.

Words, commentaries, and the conventional methods we use, as useful as they are, remain completely insufficient as the means of recognizing the truth.

> "To receive spiritual truths and to cognize the spiritual stages, one cannot depend upon reason which is rooted in matter."[5]

As long as research is focused on the surface and layers of the subject under study, the results in both the physical and metaphysical sciences will be incomplete, superficial and unreliable. True research is attained when the researcher explores and discovers all aspects of a subject where not even one point or angle is left out of his observation.

This is why knowledge of each and every single manifestation of life, of which there is an infinite number and unlimited variety, is not a logical approach to cognition of existence, for there is layer after layer to be removed and always more veils to be uncovered. It seems logical to conclude that in order to gain knowledge of existence, human beings should concentrate and focus on cognizing (knowing) each and every aspect of the only manifestation of life that is truly available to them, and that is one's own "self".

Our relationship with the external world is based on our limited sensory inputs and self-made thought processes. Sensory receptors with their bounded range only accept certain wavelengths and frequencies translated into a series of action potentials which is the language of the brain. This translation process is affected by the observer's physical and emotional condition, mood, etc. This is then stored in the brain and is based on a series of variables, which results in a perception that is nothing but one's own creation. This illusion is far from the reality of that object. This is why if one cuts an apple in half and gives one half to one person and the other half to another, the first one may describe his share of the apple as sour, while the other one claims the same apple is sweet. Is the apple sweet or sour? Neither! The reality of an apple is situated within the apple, and it is not bound to comparisons. No one can recognize that reality no matter how much research is done on the characteristics of the apple. As long as the observer and what is being observed are separated, the reality remains hidden. As Molana Shah Maghsoud Sadegh Angha has said: "We do not really hear the special tune of things, but the tune that we do hear is the tune of our own soul."[6]

So, whatever exists has specific characteristics of its own, and cannot cognize or present anything other than itself. For example, when the word "water" is expressed, it specifies certain characteristics which are only manifested in water. Although the reality it contains is inherently absolute, as soon as it is presented in a physical form and bounded to a certain state of existence, it exhibits a particular appearance reflecting characteristics of its own. The same holds true for each of us. Existence is infinite and absolute. The basis and inherent component of existence in each creature, whatever form and shape it takes, is true reality and being, which transcribes unity and singularity. To gain knowledge of this inherent reality and absolute unity, one cannot focus his research outside of himself. This is why the guiding rule that illuminates the path of all seekers from the smallest particle to far reaching galaxies is expressed in this teaching of Maktab Tarighat Oveyssi Shahmaghsoudi:

Nothing but darkness is what lies outside of you,
And nothing but light is what lies within you.

If the path of discovery is limited to superficial observation of external objects, the result will not be accurate nor will it provide the all encompassing truth which would satisfy the inquisitive soul of the seeker. It is essential for the investigator to search the depth of his own true "self", where illuminated by the light within, he will transcend to the state of gnosis and discover the truth of life.

The investigator who has gained knowledge of the reality of his own existence, has discovered religion. Thus there is no longer any doubt or hesitation. In other words, he has now established his life on the stable basis that is his true "Self", which is the only true reality and is completely free of doubt and hesitation.

As it is stated in the *Holy Qur'an (2:1-3):*

Alif Lam Mim
This is the Book; in its guidance there
is no doubt for the devout.
Those who believe in the Unseen,
Are steadfast in their prayer,
And give of what We have
Provided for them.

This is why Prophets and the Holy Saints persistently guide man to the path of self knowledge. As Imam Ali (peace be upon him) has said:

Do you not ponder that you are a microcosm?
And contained within you is the macrocosm?
And you are that Clear Book whose words
reveal the hidden.[7]

The Holy Prophet Muhammad (peace and blessings upon him) has said:

"Whoever cognizes the true self has cognized God."

One of the teachings of Socrates which was engraved on the entrance to his school was: "Know thy self." And as Hazrat Mir Ghotbeddin Mohammad Angha has said:

> It became evident that my Beloved was inside the house,
>
> All external search was nothing but idle talk and a trap."[8]

It is essential to evaluate man in the various levels of existence as he is the focus of all thought and interaction. Basically, man can be evaluated on two levels, the materialistic and the spiritual. The first includes three levels:

- the materialistic nature where physical interactions with the external world take place;
- the physical body which provides physiological and mechanical functions; and
- finally, the delicate physical body which is nurtured by either the materialistic or spiritual dimensions.

The spiritual dimension contains the core of one's being and one's true identity. Each state provides its own distinct and particular result, varying from each other. To know man, one should study him in all these dimensions and levels. Imam Ja'far Sadegh (peace be upon him) has said:

> The manifestation of man is God's greatest proof for his creatures, for he is a book which has been

created by His wisdom; he is the totality of all that exists; the straight path to all that is good, and the bridge which is drawn between heaven and hell.

For the sake of clarification, let us use the metaphor of man as a comet. His true identity is the fiery core which resembles the source of its creation. This is the heaven promised by the Prophets. The layers close to the core contain varying degrees of light, and the outer most layer is dark and in total contrast to the core. This is the materialistic nature, also referred to as hell. Hell is the unstable part of man which is in constant change, filled with demands and desires, and which is never satisfied. One who spends his life building and tending this unstable materialistic nature, satisfying each and every desire, is spending his days in darkness and ignorance. He will not benefit from the light of knowledge that is within him; and of his inherent and infinite ocean of capacities and capabilities, he would only benefit but a drop.

The reality of religion is an invitation to the journey from without to within, a transcendence from the stages of dispersion and disunity to the state of boundless unity, from the darkness of ignorance to the light of knowledge, from hell to heaven. The more one becomes entrenched in the various layers and stages that separate his limited, materialistic form from his infinite, absolute being, the more difficult it will be to become free and detached and capable of rising up to fulfill this journey.

This is why the seeker is reminded to be persistent in gathering all his energy in the focal point within him, and to repent from wasting his energy on the external world. If we pay close attention to the pattern of growth in a child, it becomes apparent that at the time of birth and for awhile thereafter, the child is compelled to spend energy in order to establish relative conformity with the world around him. This expenditure of energy through the senses allows him to gain a sense of coordination and relative adaptation with the outside world. Whether it is done out of habit or in order to achieve complete adaptation, a person who is constantly living in his external world is bound by desires and wishes. He is constantly trying to adapt himself to his environment. A new goal, a new route, a new image in his external environment attracts him and he deceives himself that achieving this new object of desire will bring him happiness and tranquility. This is a common experience.

People set up a goal that is based on social standards of status or personal gratification and spend all their effort and energy to achieve it, but when it is achieved, the gratification is momentary and the quest for happiness continues. This is because we are trying to adapt ourselves to the environment, which is ever changing and unstable. As soon as we reach a goal, our materialistic nature, which is unstable, has already changed to a new tune set by the external world. Thus, whatever energy is spent trying to build stability, tranquility, and absolute happiness based upon the unstable world is futile. In the midst of all these variables how can one reach contentment? An example which may explain this state of instability is that of a large body of water. If many outlets exist, the water is not contained. The water runs out aimlessly if there are no canals constructed to guide it, and soon the water is absorbed by the earth and the benefit of all this wealth is minimal. Soon this resource is wasted and the water is gone. The solution, we know, is constructing a dam. The same is true for human beings. Religion is the manual for constructing a spiritual dam to prevent the devastation, disintegration, and gradual consumption of our energies and inner strength by our earthly attachments and external belongings. Just as constructing a dam prevents the waste of water, controlling the five senses, correctly practicing concentration and meditation, and learning to direct all energy using our resources in a focused manner, prevents the waste of our valuable time and capabilities. "And He loves those who keep themselves pure and clean." *(Holy Qur'an, 2:222)*

Concentration of energies and inner strength on one focal point has been the practice of true scientists throughout time, and has resulted in their various discoveries. True scientists and scholars are aware that it was neither the simple fact of a falling apple nor Newton's eyes perceiving the event that caused his cognition of the law of gravity. Rather it was focusing all his energies and thought processes on one point and his momentary placement of his true "self" with its infinite wisdom that opened his inner vision to the law of gravity. In that instant in which he resided in the state of true "self", a mere action unfolding its limited appearance allowed Newton's "self" to experience and recognize the magnificent and unlimited law, hidden beyond the superficial appearances. Obviously, if it were merely the event of an apple falling from a tree, or any other object or manifestation of nature that led to the cognition of the laws of existence, many others who see these or similar events would also discover the laws of nature. This is not the case, as we all know. Depending on the perceptions of the senses does not lead anyone to the path of discovery and cognition. Eyes see but have no vision; ears hear but have no audition. As Jesus said, "Only those who have ears shall hear."

> Whatever is seen outwardly and imagined inwardly is illusion,

> Whatever is witnessed through the heart and observed externally is truth.

A very significant part of the teachings of Sufism is purification. It is obvious that a balloon carrying sacks of sand would remain attached to earth and would be unable to rise and float in the skies above, as it is intended to do. A person who is attached to earth by desires, jealousy, anger, hatred, and other cellular drives, cannot experience the boundless world within himself. Removal and separation from these attachments, and purification of one's identity from impurities results in being free from the dense, harsh physical existence, so that one may enter the kingdom of spiritual existence — the state of tranquility and survival. This is why the Holy Prophet of Islam states:

> Say: 'I am but a man like yourselves, (but) the inspiration has come to me, that your God is One God: Whoever expects to meet his Lord, let him work righteousness, and, in the worship of his Lord, admit no one as partner.[9]

One should ask himself, why is there no revelation nor any mystical inspiration for me? Why have I not experienced my metaphysical existence and realized the depth of my being? The answer was revealed in the above verse from the *Holy Qur'an*. Do you want to experience the same? Then, "...work righteousness." Cut your bondage to earth, discard all your attachments, your loads and acquisitions and be free of all else but He, so that you may admit no one in the worship of your Lord, "...admit no one as partner."

The oyster can only present the precious pearl hidden inside it after breaking through the shell. The delicate seedling blossoms from the seed only after the wooden outer layer is split. Similarly, the various layers of physical attachments, cellular desires and materialistic accumulations must detach in order for one's inherent knowledge to present itself and grow in its infinite capacity.

One of the fundamental principles in the teachings of Maktab Tarighat Oveyssi Shahmaghsoudi is the center point of one's being, which is the recipient of divine revelations and metaphysical inspirations. We have heard of the different types of concentration. Some concentrate on the area of their navel while others concentrate on a point outside of themselves, or on repeating a word or a phrase. While different temporary results may be achieved in each of these practices, none of them are unlimited or permanent. It resembles accumulating one's wealth and storing it in a bag with a hole in it; before long all that was accumulated is dispersed again. Whether it is one's navel, brain cells, visual focus on a point on the wall, or repeating words or phrases, all of these are limited and devoid of spirituality. One should concentrate on the center point of one's being which results in the blossoming of the metaphysical being and the unveiling of the infinite absolute existence.

This center is called the *source of life*. It is located in the heart and is considered the basis for all spiritual experience, revelation and interaction with existence. This focal point contains man's unlimited, unbounded knowledge. Its first function is revealed in the third week of embryonic development. Before this phase, life is exhibited in purely cellular form, in a mass of undifferentiated cells called bastula. In the third week, the first electrical pulse of life from this node initiates life in its future differentiated human form. Soon, the heart, brain, and other organs are formed. This first pulse, and every other pulse thereafter, is in harmony with existence. Consider a lamp that is connected to the source of electricity through the plug. As long as the connection is undisturbed it presents electricity in its own form. Any time that lamp wants to benefit from this unlimited, boundless electricity, it must be plugged in to it. For the human being, that point of connection, that plug, is the *source of life*. That point is constantly in harmony and in touch with existence, and the physical body and its function is dependent on this harmonious connection. The *source of life* is meant to provide life not only in the physiological level but in the metaphysical level as well. The elevation of man to his spiritual levels, what the Prophets have called the heavens or the kingdom of heaven, is through this point — the *source of life*.

What is of essence in the teachings of the School of Islamic Sufism is that if a meaning is to be revealed to man, a discovery to be made, and the reality of entities and events to be experienced as they truly are, that truth must be discovered from within oneself. That is to say, they must be inwardly known and experienced. So that man, who exists and is not separate from existence, may discover the vast and infinite existence within his own being. If man discovers the reality of his own being, all other matters will be easily known as well. It is stated in the *Holy Qur'an (4:59)*, "O ye who believe! Obey God, and obey the Apostle, and those charged with authority among you." What is considered in this verse is the totality, the source of all effusions — the Creator, God. For example, the sun is the cause and the source of the existence of the Earth and other planets who are its offspring. In whatever way or form life is manifested, it follows the laws that have emanated from the central source — the sun. These same laws govern the various evolutionary stages of lifeforms as manifested on Earth, from the particle to the human being. As long as each entity is submitted to these laws, it is able to continue its evolutionary journey of completion.

The above Holy verse indicates that God is the source of all effusions, and the Holy Prophet (the Apostle) is the one who has the capacity to receive revelation — without the interference of a personal will — from the central source. For example, the moon that is seen in the sky reflects light, but it is not the source of light. The reason it is luminous is because it is situated within the field of the sun, and is submitted to the laws governing it. If it were to be derailed from its position it would no longer be the moon as we know it. The existence of all things is contingent upon a central source. The Holy Prophet and his successors are as the moon, their being is in total submission to God and the laws of God. In other words, just as the moon is seen and is luminous because of its connection and submission to the Sun, the Prophet manifests in the same manner the light of God. The Holy Prophet's emphasis on freedom and on detachment from bonds rests on his personal conviction and experience of total annihilation in the Almighty God — the central source of all that exists. It is the return to the Origin that enables each human being to know and manifest his heavenly dimension.

What is significant in the teachings of Islam in general, and Sufism in particular, is the all-encompassing and vast central source of existence which has manifested all that exists in its varying forms and stages. All that is seen is rooted in a central source, called capability, which is infinite and abundant. If you consider the letter of the alphabet *"alif"*(ﺍ) in Arabic, you will see that it starts from one point. The *"alif"* represents the various stages of that point from where the *"alif"* started. The *"alif"* bears no resemblance to the point, yet all of its manifestations are rooted in the point.

The evolutionary course of a seed is an example that can provide insight into this topic. A seed that has the capacity for growth is planted in healthy soil. Planting of the seed is in itself an announcement of a journey that is to take place. In other words, the seed has inevitably accepted undergoing a process of evolution. Each stage during its various phases of growth — roots, stem, branches, leaves, flowers and fruit — while bearing no resemblance to the seed, is rooted in the knowledge within that seed. Each phase manifests two laws; the first is comprehensiveness, and the second is the capacity to accept and manifest the laws governing it. In conclusion, nothing could have taken place in each phase of growth had there not been that central point from which all evolved. Each one of the points in each phase of growth is at the extension of the seed or root and contains the same attributes. It makes no difference which of the points we look at, for each manifestation is a reflection of the expansive innate command which is hidden within it. Nothing can take place in any of these points of growth other than what is within its own innate nature. Should the connection be cut at any point during this process, its course of life would terminate.

To explain this process further, if we draw a perpendicular line and a horizontal line that intersect each other, the point of intersection can be considered as the location where the seed is placed in the soil. The process of growth downward and upward from the central point where the seed has been placed will show that each point along this longitudinal axis is anchored on this central point which has manifested this growth process — root and stem. Each point along this axis contains within it all the attributes that are manifested in the other phases of growth. Therefore, nothing but what is within that seed can be manifested at any point of its growth. The cause for all the manifestations that we see is the life-force (command, creator) which is unseen (hidden) within the seed and commands all the phases of growth. When it follows its innate laws and is able to move through its phases of growth, then we can say that it is one and in harmony with its own innate "command" or "creator" hidden within it. The will of each point of growth is one with the will of the central source, the "command" or the "creator". If you visualize this growth process on the longitudinal axis as I have described, it will take the form of *"Alif Lam Mim"* (الم).

Let us consider again the following verses from the *Holy Qur'an:*

> Alif Lam Mim
> This is the Book;
> In it is guidance sure, without doubt,
> To those who fear God;
> Who believe in the Unseen,
> Are steadfast in prayer,
> And spend out of what We
> Have provided for them;

If we look closely at the above verses we will see that the same law is explained — that the hidden core of all life-forms is the "Unseen" which cannot be validated through any physical experimentation, but is evident in its manifestations. When the human being follows its innate "Command", or the "Creator", he will be able to manifest the knowledge hidden within him. The human being is a book whose knowledge can be known if he is in harmony and submitted to the laws governing his being. He must rise *(ghiyam)* and endeavor, and do righteous deeds until his entire being becomes embued with the knowledge inherent in his being.

The knowledge within oneself can manifest itself on the physical life journey, or it can manifest itself on other levels. The human being's capacity for manifesting this knowledge is infinite. What prevents the human being from knowing his divinity is his attachment to his earthly appetites and desires. Life is absolute and the human being is capable of manifesting the "Absolute" within him, provided he is in balance and harmony with the source of life governing his being. When the human being is in the state of balance, he manifests "Life", therefore, his actions are rooted in the Divine Command, and cannot be but righteous. If he is in the state of carnal self, he manifests nature, and he will be subject to the laws governing nature — assimilation, absorption and dispersion.

When the Holy Prophet said, *"la ilaha ill'Allah"* (لَا إِلَهَ إِلَّا اللهُ), the first *"la"* (لَا) announces negation of self which in essence means eternal existence. It is in effect, the breaking of limitation in the unlimited Existence. When the human being exists in limitation which is his natural existence or *"Mim"* (م), his life-journey is within the boundaries of nature. He has the capacity for transcendence, but only manifests Life in the realm of nature. When his existence is founded upon *"la"*, rises *(ghiyam)* from *"la"*, and negates all earthly bonds, he is declaring Life in its absolute form.

Through self-annihilation, which is the essence of submission, he is able to manifest his eternal existence.

The reality of *"Allah"* (اللّٰه) is related to annihilation. When the Holy Prophet Muhammad (peace and blessings upon him) said *"Allah"*, it indicated his own state of annihilation in the Absolute Existence, and therefore, what he said contained guidance. Amir al-Mo'emnin Ali (peace be upon him) was close to the Holy Prophet, both physically and spiritually, and whatever the Holy Prophet said, Amir al-Mo'menin experienced, and it became reality for him, indicating that there was physical and spiritual harmony which arose from the depth of Amir al-Mo'menin's central source of existence.

The law of Islam is *"la ilaha ill'Allah"*. When each level of the human being rises *(ghiyam)* from the central source which is the life principle, it is a state of ascension for him. There are seven *alifs* within the word *"la ilaha ill'Allah"*, each representing a different stage in the creation of the human being. To journey through these seven stages, he must continuously be in a state of repentance which means total awareness or turning towards his centrality or the *qiblah*. When the human being journeys through the seven stages of his being, then he attains his divinity as "created in the image of God". When the body, the words and the heart are focused on and are founded upon the ***source of life***, all actions reflect the state of true devotion. As it is stated in the

Holy Qur'an (24:37), "Men whom neither traffic nor merchandise can divert from the remembrance of God." "All (the celestial bodies) swim along, each in its rounded course." (Holy Qur'an, 21:33)

This is why in the teachings of Sufism it is essential that each person make the journey to the source of life in order to discover the reality of his being and his place in this extensive universe.

In *The Principles of Faghr and Sufism*, Molana Shah Maghsoud has said:

> The human being's experiential and cognitive (reflective) path must ultimately lead to a method and a way, that through inward discoveries and stabilizing of mental faculties and energies, he will be able to guide himself to a point of stability and inward cognition, so that he may know the reality of objects, circumstances, and events. That is to say, developing a vision and knowledge that is so totally encompassing, that nothing remains unknown in his scope of knowledge. God, please show me the reality of things as they are.
>
> Therefore, recognizing this method of discovery, which is most crucial and at the same time the most direct method of recognition, in the sublime school of self-knowledge is considered as the essential goal for the seeker. In my opinion, the source of life in the heart, the commander and the foundation for the life activities and the mechanical aspects and the existence of the human being, has a more delicate and profound

responsibility — to lift the boundaries and limitations created by the mind which prevent the discovery of the universe beyond, and the cause of events. This method should open a special chapter in the scientific book of the world. Although the knowledge of this central source and its stages of cognition are inherent and ancient in the book of the human being, yet, they have not been the subject of inquiry and recognition except for the elevated and pure souls, who are but a few.[10]

Observation of results and presentations by the limited perceptions of the senses and imaginary deductions of the mind will not bring forth the essence of being. Only the heart and spiritual focal point can reveal the unbounded existence. It is through concentrating and recognizing all the infinite capabilities of the source of life that one can discover the absoluteness of the universe. In Sufism, the point of focus is the heart and its purification through the seven stages brings enlightenment and enrichment of the soul. The heart resembles a mirror which can reflect the light of truth once it is cleansed of the external dust that has covered it. As the Holy Prophet Muhammad (peace and blessings upon him) has said, "Knowledge is not acquired through study, but it is a light that God shines in the heart of he whom He wills."[11]

For the cognition of reality, man, the essence of existence, the most delicate of creations and the reflection of the absolute, has capabilities and instruments as boundless as creation itself. At the elevated, pure level of enlightenment, he can witness all the aspirations and glories of existence. He must free himself of the limitations of the senses. Based on the fact that in physical research and experiments sensory perceptions are unreliable, and the accuracy of the brain's imagined deductions are questionable, it is most clear that in metaphysics the senses and brain cells cannot offer useful results, nor are they considered essential.

In *The Principles of Faghr and Sufism*, Hazrat Shah Maghsoud states:

> Limitation of the senses and imagination on the one hand, isolated thinking and sensory barriers on the other, have made the human being descend from his human and heavenly elevated rank and prevented him from attaining the state of permanence of his true personality in the absolute eternal; and natural desires and tendencies have replaced his gnostic and sublime acts of devotion. The bountiful capability which is supposed to be the architect of his cognition and personality, in tending to the sensory expectations and illogical perceptions sinks in the desert of his beastly appetites and material desires. The guidance of capability in its true and constructive course, is the journey of the personality in following the path of the caravan of the martyrs and lovers of Existence, those who have always guided thirsty souls to the final purpose and ultimate goal.[12]

In order to reach the ultimate level of knowledge, which is recognizing the essence of existence and experiencing one's own reality, it is clear that superficial observations and limited sensory perceptions are not a suitable route to explore the essence of knowledge, due to their limited potential.

Thus, Sufism emphasizes concentration of all powers and energies in the heart. Harmony lies in repentance and purification from earthly habits and attachments which separate man from his inner self. When this harmony with existence is achieved in all physical and metaphysical levels, imaginary boundaries constructed by the mind collapse. Man then manifests himself in the unlimited horizon of existence and witnesses the unity of it. Only then will he know the meaning of *"la ilaha illa'llah"* — there is no other but God. Knowledge in its true meaning is the annihilation of the witness in the Witnessed, and the cognition of the unlimited after the boundaries of limitation have been lifted and the pure essence is manifest. Mist can only find its essence when it is concentrated and appears in its original form of a droplet. Once it is concentrated into a drop, it still needs the guiding wind to direct it to the ocean. The instant the drop joins the ocean, it dissolves the limitation of physical appearance and all the forces of nature that cause its minute and limited form. It annihilates in the absolute reality of itself which is water, boundless and infinite as the ocean. So too it is essential for the seeker to pass through the stages of the journey from the limited to the unlimited, so that he can witness his own reality.

Since all the efforts of scientists through time have been to improve the condition of mankind, what could be more fruitful than the cognition of man himself? Only after man achieves his infinite wisdom and boundless capacity, and recognizes his true potential, can he be of utmost benefit to himself and to others.

Endnotes

1. Angha, Molana al-Moazam Hazrat Shah Maghsoud Sadegh. (1989). *Dawn.* Lanham: University Press of America. p. 29.

2. Angha, Molana al-Moazam Hazrat Shah Maghsoud Sadegh. (1987). *Principles of Faghr & Sufism.* Verdugo City: M.T.O. Shahmaghsoudi Publications. p. 25.

3. Angha, Molana al-Moazam Hazrat Shah Maghsoud Sadegh. (1986). *Al-Rasa'el: The Light of Salvation.* Lanham: University Press of America. p. 80.

4. *From The World as I See It;* 1931.

5. *Principles of Faghr & Sufism.* p. 29.

6. Angha, Molana al-Moazam Hazrat Shah Maghsoud Sadegh. (1986). *Manifestations of Thought.* Verdugo City: M.T.O. Shahmaghsoudi Publications. p. 56.

7. *Nahj-ol Balaghah (The Teachings of Amir al-Mo'emenin Ali):* translated by Haj Seyd Ali Naghi Feyz-ol-Islam. Tehran: Entesharat Faghih, 1985. p. 215.

8. Angha, Molana al-Moazam Hazrat Mir Ghotbeddin Mohammad. (1986). *From Fetus to Paradise.* Verdugo City: M.T.O. Shahmaghsoudi Publications. p. 8.

9. *Nahj-ol Fissahah (The recorded teachings of the Holy Prophet Muhammad):* translated by Abolghassem Payandeh. Tehran: Sazman Entesharat Javidan, 1980. p. 102.

10. *Principles of Faghr & Sufism,* p. 95.

11. Angha, Molana al-Moazam Hazrat Shah Maghsoud Sadegh. (1986). *Al-Rasa'el: Al-Salat.* Lanham: University Press of America. p. 33.

12. *Principles of Faghr & Sufism,* p. 116.

Genealogy of Maktab Tarighat Oveyssi Shahmaghsoudi
(School of Islamic Sufism)®

Prophet Mohammad
Imam Ali
Hazrat Oveys Gharani*
Hazrat Salman Farsi
Hazrat Habib-ibn Salim Ra'i
Hazrat Soltan Ebrahim Adham
Hazrat Abu Ali Shaqiq al-Balkhi
Hazrat Sheikh Abu Torab Nakhshabi
Hazrat Sheikh Abi Amr al-Istakhri
Hazrat Abu Ja'far Hazza
Hazrat Sheikh Kabir Abu Abdollah Mohammad-ibn Khafif Shirazi
Hazrat Sheikh Hossein Akkar
Hazrat Sheikh Morshed Abu-Isshaq Shahriar Kazerouni
Hazrat Khatib Abolfath Abdolkarim
Hazrat Ali-ibn Hassan Basri
Hazrat Serajeddin Abolfath Mahmoud-ibn Mahmoudi Sabouni Beyzavi
Hazrat Sheikh Abu Abdollah Rouzbehan Baghli Shirazi
Hazrat Sheikh Najmeddin Tamat-al Kobra Khivaghi
Hazrat Sheikh Ali Lala Ghaznavi
Hazrat Sheikh Ahmad Zaker Jowzeghani
Hazrat Noureddin Abdolrahman Esfarayeni
Hazrat Sheikh Alaoddowleh Semnani
Hazrat Mahmoud Mazdaghani
Hazrat Amir Seyyed Ali Hamedani
Hazrat Sheikh Ahmad Khatlani
Hazrat Seyyed Mohammad Abdollah Ghatifi al-Hasavi Nourbakhsh
Hazrat Shah Ghassem Feyzbakhsh
Hazrat Hossein Abarghoui Janbakhsh
Hazrat Darvish Malek Ali Joveyni
Hazrat Darvish Ali Sodeyri
Hazrat Darvish Kamaleddin Sodeyri
Hazrat Darvish Mohammad Mozaheb Karandehi (Pir Palandouz)
Hazrat Mir Mohammad Mo'men Sodeyri Sabzevari
Hazrat Mir Mohammad Taghi Shahi Mashhadi
Hazrat Mir Mozaffar Ali
Hazrat Mir Mohammad Ali
Hazrat Seyyed Shamseddin Mohammad
Hazrat Seyyed Abdolvahab Naini
Hazrat Haj Mohammad Hassan Kouzekanani
Hazrat Agha Abdolghader Jahromi
Hazrat Jalaleddin Ali Mir Abolfazl Angha
Hazrat Mir Ghotbeddin Mohammad Angha
Hazrat Molana Shah Maghsoud Sadegh Angha
Hazrat Salaheddin Ali Nader Shah Angha

The conventional Arabic transliteration is Uways al-Qarani